Armor of Christ - Preparation and Engagement in Spiritual Warfare

Rogerio Cietto

Published by Rogerio Cietto, 2019.

ARMOR OF CHRIST – Preparation and engagement in spiritual battle

Published by Rogerio Paiva Cietto at Smashwords

INDEX

FOREWORD – MEMENTO MORI

If you wear or have ever worn a uniform, you have probably come into contact with the well-known colleague in all risky activities, Lady Death. She certainly comes to everyone, and no matter how much scientists and philosophers try to find ways to avoid this fateful encounter, the truth is that she continues to do her job, tirelessly.

In many risky activities, Lady Death accompanies the daily activity of that professional, in work with electricity, heights, flammable materials, diving, among many others. However, in the military profession we have the responsibility to voluntarily cause the death of a person, in the legal hypotheses that we can summarize here as self-defense (in times of peace) and just war (in a state of belligerence).

Please note: if the person acted in this way to defend his own life, or that of a third party (self-defense), or if the military (including partisans, private military contractors, and even mercenaries and guerrillas, in certain cases) took someone's life in a context of armed conflict (a somewhat nebulous concept today due to terrorism and criminal organizations), the person is justified before God in relation to the fifth commandment of the Church ("you shall not kill").

"You shall not cause the innocent and the righteous to be put to death" (Ex 23:7). We do not have the right or divine omniscience to judge whether a given person is innocent or righteous, so avoid this line of reasoning. However, the concrete acts that the person is practicing at that moment allow us to verify whether that particular conduct is tainted with malice and vice, capable of eliminating God's most precious gift to human beings and the most essential legal asset: life.

No father is obliged to accept martyrdom and leave his family in material and especially spiritual disarray, so there is no reason to be reluctant to act against any real and imminent threat to himself or to family members and loved ones. This is a dilemma to be faced in critical situations (to kill or to be killed?), and I hope you have resolved it in your mind right away. Acting in self-defense is neither a crime nor a sin (but be careful not to use excessive force, something that can easily happen in the heat of the moment).

Therefore, the God of mercy has an open heart for you, even though you have lived through the hell of war. Nothing you have done is a reason for God to stop loving you and wanting your salvation. Any excesses and even thoughtless attitudes can be neutralized by the sacrament of Confession. Divine love is waiting for you, but He is waiting for your heart to open so that He can make His home in you.

The paradigm of armed conflict is different from that of peacetime, very different. When people from different countries (or dissident/ revolutionary groups within a country) take up arms against each other, acting in the name of a State (or a supposed cause in which they believe), these people, during hostilities, cease to be mere citizens and are given the title of combatants, that is, they have the right (duty) to neutralize military objectives (other combatants, legitimate or not).

This is why non-military objectives (which will not bring any advantage to the war effort) should not be attacked, such as non-combatants, children, women, the elderly, homes, schools, hospitals, in short, any person or object that is not actively participating in hostilities.

In the same way, when hostilities cease, there is no longer any point in maintaining any animosity towards citizens of the opposing country. It turns out that a population marked by war takes many years to learn to forgive and to hand over all its suffering to God. A difficult and absolutely necessary task to prevent armed conflict from being reborn in the hearts and minds of those who have lost their families, homes, jobs, etc. to the horrors of war.

Is declaring war (a state of belligerence) or participating in a war considered a grave sin? The theory of just war lists the necessary requirements for a country to enter into an armed conflict:

- it must be declared and executed by a legitimate authority, without opposition from the people;

- for a good and just cause, such as self-defense, preventive action against a tyrant who was about to attack, or the punishment of a guilty enemy;

- with a reasonable chance of success;

- to achieve peace (right intention);

- when it is necessary to avoid an evil greater than the damage caused by the war; and

- as a last resort, after dialogue and negotiation have failed.

The Catechism of the Catholic Church sheds considerable light on this subject, and deserves to be read carefully.

2308. Every citizen and every government official must work to prevent war.

However, as long as "the danger of war persists and there is no competent international authority equipped with the appropriate means, governments cannot be denied the right of self-defence, once all peaceful negotiations have been exhausted."(73)

2309. The strict conditions for legitimate defence by force of arms must be carefully considered. The gravity of such a decision subjects it to rigorous conditions of moral legitimacy. At the same time, it is necessary:

- that the harm caused by the aggressor to the nation or community of nations be lasting, grave and certain;

- that all other means of ending it have proved impracticable or ineffective;

- that serious conditions of success are met;

- that the use of arms does not bring with it evils and disorders more serious than the evil to be eliminated. The power of modern means of destruction has a very serious impact on the assessment of this condition.

These are the elements traditionally indicated in the doctrine of the so-called "just war."

The assessment of these conditions of moral legitimacy belongs to the prudential judgment of those who are responsible for the common good.

The Catechism then comments on military activity, including compulsory service, especially when a state of belligerence is declared (a politically correct expression to warn people that their lives will be turned upside down for a long time):

2310 In this case, the public authorities have the right and the duty to impose on citizens the obligations necessary for national defense.

Those who dedicate themselves to the service of the country in military life are servants of the security and freedom of the people. To the extent that they carry out this task as appropriate, they truly contribute to the common good and to the safeguarding of peace.

You can be sure that a just and true God, who wants our salvation, would not place obstacles (even moral ones) so that a given nation that seeks peace and prosperity for its citizens is simply forced to accept that a tyrant from a neighboring country conquers and destroys it. We have enough examples in the Old Testament (Philistines, Egyptians, Babylonians...) that God not only accepts war, but uses it as a means to demonstrate His Power to pagan peoples, so that they may encounter the true God, one and eternal (who reigns even under the waters of the Red Sea).

However, merely confirming that a given war is just is no guarantee of success before God (or before men). Another valuable lesson from the Catechism that every person in arms needs to know in order to exercise his profession well:

2312. The Church and human reason declare the permanent validity of the moral law during armed conflicts. "Once a war has unfortunately begun, not everything becomes lawful between the belligerent parties" (76).

2313. Non-combatants, wounded soldiers and prisoners must be respected and treated with humanity.

Actions deliberately <u>contrary to the rights of peoples and their universal principles</u>, as well as the orders that command such actions, are <u>crimes</u>. Blind obedience is not enough to excuse those who submit to them. Thus, the <u>extermination of a people, a nation or an ethnic minority</u> must be *condemned as a <u>mortal sin</u>. One is morally obliged to resist orders to commit genocide.*

2314. "Every act of war which <u>indiscriminately destroys entire cities or vast regions with their inhabitants</u> is a <u>crime against God and man himself</u>, which must be condemned firmly and without hesitation" (77). One of the dangers of modern warfare is that it provides the bearers of scientific weapons, particularly atomic, biological or chemical weapons, with the opportunity to commit such crimes.

In short, war is chaos. Confusion, death and destruction. And the military, as the architect of chaos, is called upon to cause all of this in the lives of others, with profound and irreversible consequences for the whole of society. A soldier may leave from a war, but the war does not leave from a soldier. Here is the crucial point: how can you live the profession of arms without feeling hatred for those who wanted to kill you, or resentment for those you have killed?

The answer to this key question lies in an expression that, although ancient, retains a profound and universal relevance: *memento mori*. This Latin phrase means "remember that you are mortal" or "remember death". It may seem somber at first glance, but in fact it carries a powerful message of reflection, preparation and appreciation of life.

Memento mori has its roots in the philosophical and artistic traditions of the Western world, especially in the Middle Ages and the Renaissance. Artists created images and symbols that reminded people of their mortality, encouraging a life of virtue, reflection, and purpose. For military personnel, this expression serves as a constant reminder of the fragility of life and the importance of always being prepared for when it comes.

In the military environment, *memento mori* can be interpreted as a call to vigilance, discipline, and responsibility. Acknowledging mortality is not a reason to fear, but rather a motivation to act with courage, integrity, and dedication. After all, the awareness of finitude reinforces the importance of protecting oneself, one's comrades, and one's nation.

By maintaining this reminder, military personnel can cultivate an attitude of respect for life while preparing themselves to face challenges with determination. This perspective helps them appreciate each moment, honor their commitment to their mission, and maintain humility in the face of adversity.

Memento mori is more than just an old phrase; It is a philosophy that encourages living with purpose, responsibility and courage. For those who have taken on the commitment to defend their nation even at the cost of their own lives, it reinforces the importance of always being alert, valuing life and fulfilling their missions with honor, knowing that each moment is precious.

By remembering the finiteness of our existence, it is possible to find a way out of the deep causes that led to conflict, whether economic, social or ideological. Remember that on the other side of enemy lines there is also a young person hoping for a better world or a father asking God to return home.

Loving your neighbor as Jesus loved us is the sure way to find peace before, during or after periods of history troubled by violence. Death is a reminder to value life, always and everywhere, and to seek lasting peace, the peace of Christ.

Check out the powerful message we find in the Bible: "Blessed are the peacemakers, for they will be called children of God." This phrase reminds us of a special mission that all of us, regardless of the uniform we wear, can embrace: to be agents of peace in our actions and attitudes.

For example, this book was inspired by the Holy Spirit shortly after a very unexpected event in my life: I was on a mission, accompanying the troops, and after physical activity I went to take a shower. Since the place was improvised, there were no dividers between the showers, and soon another soldier also appeared to take a shower. After talking about the work, he asked me: "So, how many did you kill today?"

I immediately answered: "You don't understand, do you, warrior? We are here to fight the principalities and powers, the evil spirits that roam the world seeking to destroy souls. These people shooting at us every day are just the secretaries, not the real enemy." The Gospel needs to be proclaimed at an opportunity, even if it is between two naked and soapy men in a communal bathroom.

As soldiers, we are often called to protect, defend and maintain order. These tasks require courage and strength, but they also carry an even greater responsibility: to promote peace. After all, true strength lies not only in the ability to fight, but in the ability to seek peaceful solutions, avoid conflict whenever possible, and act with justice and compassion.

Being a "child of God" means living according to His teachings, and this includes being a promoter of peace. When we choose to dialogue, understand others, and act with integrity, we are reflecting God's love and mercy. Our role is not only to protect people from external threats, but also to create an environment where peace can flourish, even in difficult times.

Remember that every action you take can be an instrument of peace. Whether in your daily routine, on missions, or in your relationships with colleagues and civilians, your stance of peace and respect can transform environments and inspire others to also seek harmony.

So, dear soldier, as you fulfill your mission, remember that promoting peace is one of the greatest expressions of strength and courage. And by doing so, you will be living up to the promise of being called a child of God, reflecting His love and peace in this world.

May you continue to be a light of hope and peace, always guided by the values that strengthen not only your mission, but also your spirit. I hope this reflection is useful and inspires you to always keep this memory alive in your daily actions.

INTRODUCTION

"Contend, Lord, with those who contend with me; fight against those who fight against me", Psalms 34 (35), 1

Christian, are you ready for battle? I'm not talking about combating men of flesh and blood. These are also dangerous, and it's important to be ready against those who want to make you harm, that's for sure. It's about another battlefield. The struggle against the devil may take place on the spiritual battlefield, but the evil sends several secretaries of flesh and blood from its many combat echelons in order to disturb the life of the Christians. The camouflage is impeccable, weapons of any kind, caliber and configuration. It uses even chemical and biological weapons (didn't get it? Crack and AIDS are some) and nobody accuses it of war crimes. Its tactics challenge strategists like Clausewitz, Sun Tzu, Napoleon or Patton. Are you ready for THIS kind of combat?

I thought I were. I went to mass, confessed once in a while, tried to say the truth, pay my bills, be a good father and husband. I prayed the Rosary before the exams for a public career and was approved, even though I studied many unnecessary subjects. I did fasting to find an apartment close to my kids' school. I asked God to delay the takeoff of a plane until I arrive at the airport and miraculously my plea was answered. I even went to praying groups according to the Catholic Charismatic Renewal. But the enemy used many breaches, and attacked the moment my guard was low. These few words are a testimony of divine grace and mercy, and an effort so that others learn with my mistakes. Saint Paul wrote to Timothy: "I have fought the good fight, I finished the race, I kept the faith". So, what kind of fight is that, in which at the end of the career the person did not lose faith nor hope? More important, how to prepare and engage in this good fight?

Who has been in the physical battlefield knows very well (or should know) that the combat begins at the spiritual level, continues at the spiritual level and ends at the spiritual level. It's easy to realize that during the training. The psychological preparation to do operational courses demands from the student a goal, an objective. Nobody will make himself suffer only because of the suffering, for masochism. The students motivated by the vanity of saying "I am good!", for an increase in payment or to transmit his anger to someone may eventually complete the course, with a lot of effort, but that suffering brought no personal grow, and he learned nothing about spiritual warfare. These do not go far.

The physical preparation dissociated from the spiritual is not enough for the soldier to not despair and flee as soon as he feels the smell of blood mixed with mud and powder. In order to accept risking his life, the soldier needs total conviction that he is fighting for a good cause (promising virgins in paradise is not enough for those who have discernment) that his actions are part of a common effort to do good. The fight for his country is on the outside, but from the inside everybody fights for his family, his friends, for the life and freedom of himself and all his beloved ones. This is love for the country, real patriotism (patriotism may arise in an international sport competition, but with low intensity; that becomes clear when there's a defeat and the player suffers hostility; besides the egoism that demonstrates lack of patriotism, because the egoist doesn't want to sympathize with the loser, even when the defeat is justifiable; anybody can show solidarity when gaining, but only those who love their country can show solidarity on the losses). Another example, the war against drugs or terrorism is impersonal and doesn't motivate anybody, but if the combatant visualize the amount of drugs or fear that he can take away from his dear ones, he goes to fight with full force. True patriotism is love for the family.

Lacking moral values, the soldier can also go to battle with evil in his heart. Possessed by the devil, the combatant will win many fights, but favoring the malign, and commit atrocities against women, children and defenseless people. If that is the case, you may close this book. Do not waste your time. I refuse writing to you. Come back only after a good repent, reconciliation and conversion.

If there are no moral values to justify the battle, the soldier loses his motivation. His own conscience starts questioning: "What was I thinking?" "Am I doing the right thing?" The emotion and the adventure soon give place to tiredness and fatigue. At first contact (baptism of fire) despair takes the reins of the combatant's life, who doesn't want to die in vain, doesn't want to sacrifice himself for something that's not worth his blood.

Every battle is spiritual. If you are not ready, you have already lost. Saint Paul wrote how we should be prepared, at the Letter to the Ephesians, 6, 13-17:

"Therefore put on the full armor of God, so that when the day of evil comes, you may be able to stand your ground, and after you have done everything to stand firm. Stand firm then, with the <u>Belt of Truth</u> buckled around your waist, with the <u>Breastplate of Righteousness</u> in place, and with your <u>feet fitted with the Readiness</u> that comes from the gospel of peace. In addition to all this, take up the <u>Shield of Faith</u>, with which you can extinguish all the flaming arrows of the evil one. And take the <u>Helmet of Salvation</u> and the <u>Sword of the Spirit</u>, which is the word of God".

Preparing for the physical combat is very different than the spiritual preparation, but the basis for a good physical training is a good spiritual training. Training only the carcass may be vanity, pride or even greed, and it won't last long, or will be used for the evil to disseminate darkness, with your sins and of those who follow you. Do you want to lead other people to the dark path? Do you want to be occasion of fall for your brothers and sisters?

Certainly you have realized the use of many military expressions and slangs in this book. Don't worry. The divine things are simple, therefore I'm writing the simplest possible way, without losing content. No lucubrating or scamming. If you, however, are a professional of arms and you're not ready for the spiritual warfare, read carefully what I'm writing. The best time to read is when you're in a mission abroad, your wife and kids are sad or angry with you and your absence, and your colleagues call you to go bagging, go punching, go to the lane... You may think I'm crazy, that this book is nonsense, but read it to the end. Your family appreciates it.

What is the most pleasant part of the mission? Surely it's not the preparation, all the expectation and anxiety, preparing and testing the material, equipment, uniform, study of the area of responsibility, mission mandate, enemy, neutral and allied forces, and the pressure from the higher rank until embarking... Neither is all the tension during each patrol, the angry looks of the population, the sweat, dust and disgusting smell, from burned tires, urine, feces, the shoots that all of a sudden come from each and every place... The patrol spends the whole night climbing up and down the vehicle, and finds nothing. The Search Warrant takes a lot of time to come, and in the end the place is clear. All that considering only the previewed events. When the allegations of Human Rights and International Humanitarian Law arrive, tortured people, raped, children mutilated women, and the population is openly hostile against the troop, using sticks and stones, the escalation of violence seems to never end. So, is there any pleasure on the mission?

I can tell for myself, what I fell in my heart. The greatest pleasure of the mission is not when it ends, because I love very much what I do, and if I do my job well, and don't get rocks and stones from the population (shots from hostile forces is all right, it is previewed in the Rules of Engagement) I'm satisfied and ready to do it again, as many times as necessary. I like so much what I do that I went too far, I was so addicted to the adrenaline of combat that I volunteered for a mission abroad even against my wife's opinion. Firstly I asked for the healing of this addiction, praying the Divine Mercy Chaplet every day in front of the Holy Eucharist. Then we discussed a lot and we both made adjustments in our professional careers, in order not to trouble the family. But the joy in the end of the mission is an instant pleasure, that may come back with less intensity when we tell the events (blockades, ambushes, rescues, every person has a story to tell). So, is this all?

What fulfills my heart of joy is to come back home, receiving hugs and kisses of the children, the wife, asking how the mission was, if I'm fine, how many days off... The soldier needs to give a lot of love to his family, being present, having time available for them. On the other hand, the wife and children need to support the soldier during the mission, not ruining his emotional and keeping the cohesion. Many suicides and other forms of violence committed by the military in campaign arise from personal problems (ending a relationship or marriage, and also children disobedience). The family bonds need to be continually strengthened with joint activities and prayer, a lot of prayer, for during the mission it is very easy to be selfish and think only in the absence that the soldier will be. Nevertheless, the soldier must value up his family, strengthen the bonds, be a lot of time with them, present in body and soul, ask willingly how things are, homework, playing with the kids without shame (you can also play war games), fixing electronic appliances, offer help in domestic activities... Being present is your greatest present.

Family is everything. If you don't have a family to come back when the mission ends, then who did you fight for?

1. VIGILANCE

"Unless the Lord builds the house, its builders labor in vain. Except the Lord keep the city, the watchmen wake but in vain", Psalms 126 (127), 1.

What does it happen with the soldier when he is not vigilant during his watch, as a sentinel? He is charged with a disciplinary transgression or even a crime, if the was being lazy, no boot, weapon of the side, no head cover. All that because the enemy comes on the most unexpected moment, he doesn't come with sirens and sending fireworks (if he does, it's in your direction, not high up). Because of an unvigilant (or lazy) colleague, the entire shift pays for it: go to mud, go to water, Seated 1, 2! On your feet 1, 2!, For push-ups 1, 2! Parade training on the asphalt at 12 hours, so the sun enlighten your conscience (or to melt your brains...). If the physical combat is like that, why would it be different in the spiritual combat?

For those who are already off the boat the evil one makes no effort. After all, you voluntarily joined the ranks of evil. On the other hand, who is still on the good fight, with God and for His Glory, will suffer the charge. Those who deserted the evil ranks and is today with God is a preferential target, because he can fall again and is already infiltrated. What are the tactics, techniques and procedures, or *modus operandi*) of the enemy? Try to identify some of these in your daily life:

- pornography on the computer, at the quarters, at the workplace, on the cell phone;

- invitation to activities forbidden for the family (bar, dancing club, weed parties, etc);

- hoaxes and gossips about celebrities, shameful facts about people you know;

- people showing off about their sexual adventures, easy-earned money, obtaining illegal or immoral advantages;

- situations that help breaking the law, from IR false information to park the car in a prohibited spot;

- songs and videos making apology of crime, use of drugs, free sex, unjustified violence, in sound trucks, car sounds in high volume or cell phone web-cam videos;

- omitting the truth or lying, as a way to save yourself of doing good, as the propaganda of some Brazilian politicians;

- propaganda with subliminal messages (the attractive woman doesn't come with the beer, the cigarette, nor the luxury car advertised);

- news with a tendency to bring hate or fear in certain segments of the population.

Therefore, guarding against the traps of the evil is to go living in a desert island? Negative. You can even go to Siberia, if you take all that pollution in your head it won't make a difference. Guarding is to recognize the malignant is attacking, and repel that attack. Consider attentively if that information, image or object of consumption is important to you, if it will make you get closer to God. It's nonsense saying to yourself: "I'll be indulgent to my friends, I'll share the beer so that they don't suffer so much", "I'm going to use some drugs to get closer to the addicted, gain their trust and then lead them away from the addiction", you are lying to yourself. "Jesus didn't exclude the prostitutes, so I'll get closer to them and use their services" is one of the worst arguments to justify a serious sin, because it is a blasphemy and a distortion of the words of Jesus, an even more serious sin.

In spiritual battles the damage inflicted is painful and difficult to fix. Who saw pornography his entire life will see every woman as an object of consumption, not as a human being. And the images will be saved in privileged places of the memory, like a quick-draw holster, and come back to mind at the first opportunity. Little by little the pleasure with his own wife goes down, and during the moments away from home the instincts rise. Results: divorces, unplanned/unwanted children, bitterness and sadness for all. During missions abroad come the human rights violations, that means, the soldiers that were there to defend the population are taking advantage of the defenseless and attacking those who they were supposed to protect.

Which God do you adore? The One and All-Mighty God? You will reflect the Light of God in your life, wherever you are. Nonetheless, if your god is your body, your work, your intellect, your car, house or cellphone, or drugs, sex, violence, you are away from the true God. Come back while there's still time.

Who surrenders to his passions like the horse and the donkey, over them the devil has power, said the angel Raphael to Tobias. It's not just about sex, but also earning money, spending money, excessive and obsessive care with the body, demonstration of authority, even speaking without measure can make you a soldier of the evil, taken by greed or vanity. In the end, friend, you will be alone, with nobody to ask for help.

Without vigilance the boat is adrift, without a path. Without a family the person is unprotected, loose in the world. On the contrary, a family fearful to God is cohesive, one helps the other in difficult times. Do you want to find whom to trust? Ask your friends from the soccer or the bar if they can help you pay your credit card bills...

2. BELT OF TRUTH

"Send out thy light and thy truth, let them lead me; let them bring me unto thy holy hill, and to thy tabernacles" Psalms 42 (43), 3

The basis for a good armor is the belt, that holds it and keeps it adjusted. It's not the protection for the feet, I'll talk about this soon. A soldier without an adjusted belt cannot combat. His trousers keep falling, his vest keeps opening. He cannot run, his legs get tied in. He cannot use his legs, they are busy. He cannot carry much weigh, they are busy. How can a person combat while holding his trousers? In brief, a warrior without a belt is caught by the enemy in "short legs", showing his underwear, that uses his vulnerability and also humiliates him for his defeat.

During High School my classmates invented a joke of very bad taste: because the trousers and shorts had only a rubber band at the waist, one pulled the other's trousers in the middle of the laboratory, in front of the girls. The *bullying* only stopped when the shop started selling trousers with a string.

During a certain camp one of the soldiers had lost the belt's buckle, and got into trouble when everybody was called to go to the meeting point. When he was holding the trousers he dropped the rifle. When he was taking the rifle, the cap dropped. Fortunately we found another belt before he goes into the water and lose his trousers (or get drowned and be found dead showing his underneath). Go to battle without a belt is certain defeat.

With lies and hidden information there happen the same things.

When the person is caught lying, soon comes the sensation of shame and humiliation, as if somebody has dropped his trousers in the middle of the street, or when the trousers rip right at the crotch when you get down to grab something. There come the accusations: "Didn't you say you were at your friend's house?" "Wasn't that money spent with medicine?" ... The spiritual battle ends even before it starts, and the enemy makes a real psychological campaign to taint your image and credibility.

Who doesn't wear the belt of truth will use the lie as a weapon, or omit some important information. He hides from the family where he has been, what he did, how much he earned, how much he spent. Some even hide where they live from their colleagues, or their paycheck from the wife. The truth, my friend, protects you from the most cunnings snares of the enemy, that may hit you when you are off guard.

Another occasion of lying is the showing off of something that you are not. Personal photos in social media show people always happy, rich and powerful. It doesn't show any fights or suffer of the person, only from others. It shows the beverage, but never the hangout at work the next day. It shows the luxury car, but misses the overdue credit card bill and expenses with fuel, taxes, insurance. Nobody needs to be rich and powerful to be happy. Showing off something that you are not is even worse. Besides, when masks fall, humiliation beats all people involved. Marriages and friendships based on *status*, money or power don't last long, mistrust come up sooner or later. If it is showing off, accusations begin from all sides. No need to find who's guilty, because in this game nobody is innocent. Who lied and who expected undue advantage.

A little lie pulls another, and so on, in a chain that pulls you to the bottom. Lied? Assume it, repent it, confess it. It will hurt a lot less, and you can regain trust with time. The combatant's reputation protects a lot more than helmets or armor. Those who does evil stay in the darkness, taught Jesus, because he doesn't want his actions to be exposed. Who does good doesn't fear the Light of God, the Truth. Let the Light of God illuminate your procedure, speaking and writing with fairness and responsibility.

Courage is needed to announce the word of God, because you can be sure that every good action you do will have a retaliation. In order to protect from fear and shame, have your Belt of Truth always adjusted, always speaking with rectitude and in good time.

3. BREASTPLATE OF RIGHTEOUSNESS

"Defend the weak and the fatherless; uphold the cause of the poor and the oppressed" Psalms 81 (82), 3.

The breastplate is an armor of metal plates, assembled in order to protect the body without limiting the movements. It protects the whole body, except the head. It protects from all kinds of impact in battle, except arrows and darts (those can pierce the plate, and to take it from the body it is needed to rip a good piece of flesh with it. Nowadays the body protection is made of Kevlar and aramid plates, a lot lighter and capable of resisting firearms shots..

Well adjusted to the body the breastplate protects against impacts. If it's loose the attacks may come from the open spots (usually on the trunk, below the arms) and the combatant will run clumsily, bouncing the entire stuff. If it is too tight, the combatant gets suffocated and his movements become limited, incapacitating him to battle.

It's easy to understand the use of the breastplate of righteousness when used with the belt of truth: it's not enough to tell the truth, have an honest and sincere speech, but the truth must be combined with practice, with honest and sincere attitudes. In other words, righteousness is to doing as truth is to saying.

Well adjusted to the spirit, the armor protects against blasphemies. A fair person doesn't fall on the confidence trick, doesn't buy prized lottery tickets, doesn't participate in pyramid business schemes (Telex Free, Ostrich Master, Am Way, everyday there's a new one), doesn't access suspicious *links* sent by e-mail, doesn't make illegal water or energy connections, respects the traffic signs, respect the neighborhood regulations and laws. A fair person gives back undue or in excess payments, disposes its garbage in a proper place (he doesn't mix banana peels and batteries), he gives back objects he found, no matter the value, he respects the time of scheduled events and accomplishes his obligations.

When the theory is disconnected from the practice, everybody suffers the consequences: time is lost, money is wasted, unnecessary sorrow. Not just for the person, but for everyone around him or who believe in him. If loose, the breastplate of righteousness doesn't protect the vital points, and the enemy will use a moment of distraction; if too tight, the person becomes inflexible, with a code of conduct so high that only him (or even him), can accomplish, he becomes an irritating person, the others abandon him, and many times he is incapable of forgiving.

I wasn't always a fair person. With and speech of morality, austerity with the domestic bills, effort at work and studying, but in practice I was lazy at work, lost perseverance with the studies, spent in secret what the domestic budget didn't allow, and also was watching pornography on the computer. Of course I was hit, my flanks were unprotected. But God, in his Eternal Patience, took me out of the mud, showing my fragilities. I am still feeble in many spiritual points, but now I know where they are, and I protect them better.

It's not at all easy to be fair. It never was, and don't expect that one day it will be easy to wear the breastplate of righteousness (fairness is heavier to the spirit than the aramid vest for the body. Doubt it? Be fair and you will feel it). Know that the effort is worthy, the just person is protected from almost all attacks of the enemy (there's also the shield, we will come to it soon).

How do I know if I am being fair? Use the Golden Rule, established in International Humanitarian Law: "Don't do to others what you don't want others do to you". Don't want to be shot in the back? Don't shoot in the back. Don't want to be captured and then tortured? Don't torture. Don't want your house to be invaded and your things taken? Don't invade other people's houses (except in flagrant crimes, a disaster or a judicial warrant, and don't take other people's things (except on the cases established in law, I know you understood it). Even if the enemy does it, you shouldn't do, because the soldier of Christ keeps His words with his own life, he isn't a unscrupulous mercenary.

You may realize the Golden Rule from IHL is inspired of the words of Jesus: "Love the others like you love yourself". Jesus simplified a lot our lives, it doesn't need much effort, and doesn't come with the sad story that today things are more complicated than two thousand years ago, because the words of Christ are actual, and it will always be. Ask for discernment (your consciousness) Listen the Holy Spirit talking to you. If you don't hear anything, be careful. Be fair to yourself and the ones next to you. Or else, how can you ask God to be fair to you?

4. SANDALS OF READINESS

"Direct my steps according to thy word; and let no iniquity have dominion over me". Psalms 118 (119), 133.

Depending on the Bible you use, the translation of "Sandals of Readiness" may change, and that required me a lot of patience and discernment. I've researched the text in several languages, in order to get to a conclusion. The text on Ephesians 6, 15 may be "preparing for the Gospel of Peace", "getting ready for the Gospel of Peace" or "zeal to propagate the Gospel of Peace". Readiness is to be ready, prepared, dressed up, and soon you will understand why I've chosen "Sandals of Readiness".

Mobility is essential for the combatant. Who stays still in a battlefield becomes an easy target. In Armed Conflicts of old the fighter needed to move between trenches, or seeking shelter wherever possible, but always moving, advancing or retreating with the troop, or eventually alone.

Modern Armed Conflicts demands even more mobility, patrols on foot frequently close to civilian people, in urban environment, looking for targets and mainly to transmit trust and credibility, so as to gain the population's support. No doubt the exposure to risk is higher, but the objective is to show safeness. If the troop goes around on the middle of the street always protected inside armored vehicles, what the population will think? If the troop doesn't feel safe, even less the civilians. And when the vehicle breaks the asphalt, the pedestrian walkway, the parked cars, the people's feet, the shot backfires, and those who should guarantee a safe and secure environment becomes hostile. Wallowed in the mud, soldier!!!

Item in the backpack of every combatant is the antiseptic for the feet, usually in powder. It is used to avoid that a ringworm, a callus or athlete's foot take the fighter out of action. He will not only leave the fight, but take two other fighters to transport it, which may compromise the mission. The feet need to be protected from all kinds of natural dangers (humidity, cold, heat, thorns, roots, snakes) or man-made ones (stumbling line, anti-personal mines, traps).

Did you realize the importance of movement and the protection of the feet on the battlefield? The spiritual warfare involves the same movement. A Christian doesn't fight any enemies in front of the television, except watching preaches and programs that announce the Word of God, and even that is little. A combatant of Christ has to leave home and use his feet a lot in order to help the different tasks of the Parish, for example distribution of food for families in need, help the kermesses and celebrations, among other activities that require fast and confident feet.

Out church is pilgrim. Doing pilgrimages is equivalent to pray with the feet (remember that on your next march). Jesus did two pilgrimages as soon as he came to the world, one in his mother's womb to Bethlehem, and another to Egypt, due to Herod's' rage. As an adult, Jesus did his trips on foot, in order to be in touch with the people. For a pilgrimage you need to protect and take care of your feet.

How to do this foot care on the spiritual field? Being always ready to announce the Gospel. Get up from the sofa and seek the closest parish. Offer the help you can, not just money. The churches need proactive people, that make it happen, that bring the light of God to the neighbor.

One of the most exciting programs that my family and I did together was to distribute food to homeless people, with the group of our parish. No one was excluded, it was a family activity, and brought all of us closer. In a Friday night, instead of going to a restaurant to be served, we served a hot meal for people who don't know if they will eat the next day. It was unforgettable . We even ate with them, in the end.

Woe to me if I do not preach the Gospel, wrote Saint Paul. In order to engage in this kind of combat, my brother, you need to be in readiness and take the opportunities that arise. What's the use in having the light of God if you waste it, illuminating no one? It's not enough to know the Gospel, you need to bring it to those who are in the darkness.

In Matthew, 8: 8, it is narrated that a centurion (equivalent to a Captain in modern military hierarchy) asks Jesus to save his servant. When Jesus asks to go to the servant, the centurion says: "Lord, I do not deserve to have you come under my roof, but just say the word, and my servant will be healed". The centurion continues: "For I myself am a man under authority, having men under me: I tell this one: Go, and he goes; and to another: come, and he comes". The centurion was ready for whatever Jesus decided do to about the subject, in total submission, and also let clear that if Jesus only said: Go, the sickness would leave; or say: Come, and the healing would come immediately. In combat it is similar, when the commander calls your name, you have to be ready for whatever is needed, and follow the orders, without hesitation or sloppiness.

Still didn't get it, Christian? When Jesus says: go deliver some food to a person in need, you go, no wondering, no delaying, be it raining, snowing or sunny. When Jesus says: come to a poor community to help, you come, as a disciplined warrior, aware of your duties as a Christian. When Jesus says: do a spiritual retreat or a pilgrimage, you answer like Mary, example of obedience: "Behold, I am the servant of the Lord, let it be to me according to your word". When Jesus calls your name, you answer: I'm ready, Commander! UNDERSTOOD!?!?!?

5. SHIELD OF FAITH

"You who fear him, trust in the Lord; he is your help and shield", Psalms 114 (115), 11

Before the invention of firearms the shield was an essential part of every warrior. Blunt, piercing or slashing blows could be stopped, bringing a tactical advantage that can make a difference. The shield is held on the weak arm, because the strong one will hold a weapon. The larger the shield, the bigger the protection, but the heavier it is the less is the agility in the battlefield.

Nowadays the shield is used only in crowd control (public manifestation of violent groups) or in tactical entrances, when a person is locked in a place and resisting prison/capture.

The modern combatant also needs a good amount of faith (that the parachute will open, that the weapon won't jam, that the fuel will be enough, that the enemy will lose the shot), but the most important faith is in God, deliver yourself to His Will with altruism and self denial, fearing God and not the enemy, be it physical or spiritual. Even if you do everything right in your life, be truthful and just every time and every place, the enemy will attack you. Even without any breaches with lies or unfairness, the attacks will come.

Does the Christian need a shield of faith? You probably have noticed that the breastplate of righteousness protects against many attacks of the enemy. But not all of them, because when the enemy doesn't find any breach on the life of the just person, he comes with full throttle, to put the combatant down in any way, with a frontal charge, that the sandals of readiness won't be able to dodge. To the fighter the only thing left is to group up and receive the charge with hope and no muttering, like Job, a just man that suffered all kinds of misfortune, and did not sin against God.

I'll give an example. My car was parked accordingly, during the day, and when I came back to it somebody crashed so hard on its side that it that it went up the pedestrian walk. Loss of a few thousand reais.

Did I do anything wrong to deserve that punishment? It's not up to me to know the divine intentions, but in that situation there was nothing unfair in my conduct. The only thing left to do was to call the insurance company (the person who crashed the car left a phone number, and fortunately his insurance covered all expenses).

In this situation when the unfair impact (at least apparently) hits the person, many times the reaction is of fury or despair, blaspheming against God and the world. "What did I do to deserve that?", "It's not possible, why me?", "God wanted it", and other infamies. Many just people end up quiting everything because they weren't able to receive a frontal attack from the enemy, and fell on sin. Symptom of lack of faith.

However, the Christian that keeps his Shield of Faith well polished and shining, takes the blow with no faint. Did they clone your credit card? Lost your job? Pick-pocketed your cell phone? Had a flat tire while going to the job interview? Had diarrhea or colic on the day of your university admission exam or public job test? Your daughter prostituted herself? Your son got involved with drugs? Your husband is in adultery? Your wife abandoned the house and the kids? There's no use in getting away from your responsibilities, accusing others just to exempt yourself. Be fair in everything, denounce, fight for your rights. But when justice is over, receive the impact with a lot of faith, keep going forward and open way amidst the fire with your Shield of Faith, without turning back on the way, like a warrior that fears God should behave.

I left the best example to the end. The trial of Jesus wasn't not even a little fair, and even so he received the flagellation and martyrdom without muttering against God. During his crucifixion he even sang Psalm 21: "My God, my God, why have you forsaken me?" The whipping and the nails may have perforated his body, but his confidence was always intact, his emotional condition remained the same, without any manifestation of lacking hope, of despair. Jesus was absolutely certain, without a speck of doubt, that he would overcome death. Otherwise, how could he forgive his executioners and keep a respectful dialogue with God, being nailed to the Cross?

Having a Shield of faith doesn't mean that the combatant will never fall in sin, but he will have the faith, the necessary strength for the Christian to get up and face the adversities. Even if you have followed accurately the azimuth, trained and followed the Commandments in full, if the parachute doesn't open, the weapon jams, the fuel ends or the enemy hits the target, deliver to God your life and embrace your destiny with joy in your heart.

"If your body can't endure, it's your faith that ensure!"

6. HELMET OF SALVATION

"Lord, I have hoped for thy salvation, and done thy commandments", Psalms 118 (119), 166.

The weakest part of the body is the head, essential for the survival of the entire body. Head injuries are irreversible in most cases. The warriors of erstwhile wore metal helmets, with a small opening in front for the eyes and breathing, and a signal indicating the troop they belonged, usually a big and colorful feather, in order to avoid fratricides.

Modern combatants wear ballistic helmets, capable of protecting the head from firearms hits. Who has used a combat helmet knows how it bothers, besides the sweat and headache, and possible baldness due to prolonged use. But the head needs to be protected, because a shot can cause instant death.

In the same manner, the helmet of salvation protects the combatant in the place where he is most vulnerable: the thoughts. It's not easy to enter in a direct confrontation with a determined Christian and firm in his faith: therefore, the enemy uses indirect means, so as to confuse the fighter's thoughts and disorient him.

How does this tactic work? Also called subversion war, the enemy tries to create rebellion in the person intimacy, turning it relative everything he believes, his moral values, culture and traditions. That way the combatant ends up fleeing the battlefield, he deserts or asks to leave his unit (his family) and lives errantly, with no route on the world, and is easily co-opted by the adverse forces.

The enemy's propaganda aims to destroy the values that strengthen the combatant's faith: corruption and favoritism decrease the values of work and entrepreneurship; adultery weakens the importance of the family, paternity and maternity; lying as a way to get rid of problems or escaping from responsibilities is advertised as a solution, whereas honor and truth are seen as hindrances, obstacles to achieve an objective; stimulation to exaggerated and precipitated consumption makes the person covet more and more material goods, forgetting charity and love to the people in need (when charity has second intentions it becomes a favor exchange).

The attack is very strong also by vanity, and without realizing it men and women are inclined to worship their bodies like if they were gods, sacrificing their health and shortening their lifetime with drugs and surgeries. Boasting about academic titles, positions of importance in companies and public institutions is an example of vainglory. And as if all that wouldn't be enough, those who bends to vanity or vainglory, put are not able to put it into practice, gets envy and nourish their rage with robberies and assassinations.

Nothing of that is new, they are capital sins for millennia, but the psychological campaign of the enemy is exactly to make the person believe that there are situations, in the modern world, that justify the perpetration of these sins. "The important thing is to be happy", "If I don't take care of myself, who will?", "I'm giving a gift to myself, I deserve it", "Everybody does, why wouldn't I do it?" are unjustifiable excuses. It may take a few hours or several years, the combatant's faith gets worn out by watching soap operas, reading sensationalist news, immoral movies, frequent places that make easy having sex without compromise, or live among people that practice those sins.

How, then, should the Christian protect himself from these attacks, that little by little falter their faith? Remembering the reason that rule our lives. Ask yourself: for what reason do we fight so much in this world, for our lives, for our family? It's an endless fight to work honestly every day, keeping the good humor, give attention to the wife, talking with the kids. Taking some food to a community in need is a struggle of war. Visiting an orphanage, then, is a hostage rescue operation. It's a lot easier to sin. So, why so much weariness?

To be saved, of course. Christian, your objective is to be saved, the eternal life. Therefore, remember that everything that you do in this life, do it thinking on what would be God's will for you. But be honest to yourself, ask advice from people that are close to you and also to Him.

Many times I suffer this dilemma: my activity requires that, from time to time, I follow the troops during missions, at places in conflict or in humanitarian crisis, in the homeland or abroad, in order to instruct the soldier about the legal aspects of the mission (Human Rights, International Law of Armed Conflicts, Rules of Engagement and Norms of Conduct) and investigate the cases of misconduct. This activity fills my heart with joy, I feel I'm being useful to the troop, to the civilian population, and specially to God, because my activity helps restoring the dignity of the human being, very often ignored due to the heat of the battle.

However, when helping others, I need to sacrifice the time dedicated to my family, because I spend several weeks and even months to away from home. In order to attenuate my temporary absence, I try to talk on the phone or by video-conference (praying too), I ask them to send homework by e-mail for me to correct, I ask about school, we play guess what. I miss them immensely. It's necessary a lot of discernment to understand what is the desire of God for me, if I should help people flagellated by wars or catastrophes, or to comply with my duties as husband and father.

After a lot of praying and talking with a number of priests, military chaplains, Christian colleagues from the military and my family, I got to the conclusion that both can be God's Will, leaving the soldier with the task of dividing adequately his time between work and family, and in the case of deadlock the family's value is higher. More important, however, is to follow your conscience. If you are going to the mission just for the money, or to escape from your family obligations, you can stop this very moment. Make a good confession, a good penance in push ups and kangaroo jumps, and come back to read this book from the beginning.

The helmet of salvation will help you remember always and in any place what your mission is, to do God's Will, and your objective, which is to be saved. You cannot let the rhetoric of the enemy to hit you. During the missions we are more vulnerable emotionally, due to anxiety, combat stress, lack of comfort, etc. Without the Helmet of Salvation there comes the discussions for futilities, jealousy, egoism, arrogance, and the higher mission (to save your soul) is compromised, as much as the smaller missions (to rescue and protect the population, arrest criminals, neutralize enemy combatants).

Many soldiers commit suicide because they are emotionally shaken, thoughts of suffer and death torment his head day and night, memories of people in absolute misery, buried in rubble or another casualty take away his sleep. Colleagues committed suicide during operations overseas because his wife finished the relationship and told him by phone. Wives, know well your husbands prior to make extreme decisions like those. If they are hopeless tramps or cheaters, a divorce will not have a great impact on the short term (remorse comes with time), and they will not kill themselves. However, if they are good people, fearful to God, but immature, incapable of shielding their emotions, the chance of suicide is much higher. The same goes to the husbands, when the wife is in a mission away from home.

Do you remember all I wrote in the first chapter, about vigilance and not letting the pollution of the world to get into your head? Clean all that dirt and fill it with memories of your families, from adventures during trips to playing after dinner. Your designation to the mission will be well received by everyone. Above all, remember: if you are not fighting for your salvation, then what are you fighting for?

7. SWORD OF THE SPIRIT

"So shall I answer them that reproach me in any thing; that I have trusted in thy words", Psalms 118 (119), 42.

Since Bronze Age pre-historical combatants used swords of diverse formats, sizes and weighs. Each civilization has manifested its own style, and because of that the Japanese *katana* is so different from the Muslim scimitar, the Iberic greatsword or the Roman gladius. Even with the invention of firearms, the sword is still a symbol of the honored and fair combatant.

Black powder, and later the grooves in the barrel, changed the battlefield. Earlier the close combat distance was two meters, now it is two hundred or more. A combatant many times does not know who hit him or from where, the technologies applied in combat brought a significant boost in the last century, increasing the lethality of the armed conflicts.

However, it is still forbidden conducts that cause unnecessary suffer or excessive damage to the combatant, like explosive or expansive ammunition, laser weapons that cause permanent blindness, anti-personnel landmines. Chemical, biological and radiological weapons are also prohibited, because they do not distinguish between legitimate targets (combatants) and others (civilian population).

The use of the sword (or the rifle, nowadays) is the *métier* of the combatant. All training and equipment is suited for him to use his weapon in the best conditions, aiming to neutralize the enemy. That is why the most important step of training is the use of the weapon. Assembling, disassembling, maintenance, adjusting, use of crosshairs, shooting without aiming, shooting when decumbent, knelt, standing, loading, changing weapon in combat, progression, covering and sheltering, shooting with night vision goggles, with spyglass, thermal vision, tracing or piercing ammo, that is the everyday of the combatant, including the Christian combatant. In combat, the rifle is the girlfriend, it needs to be taken good care of it, protecting it, always at the shoulder even to take a shower, it has to sleep embraced to the rifle as to a wife, but keep it locked in order to avoid an accidental shoot (this also applies to dating before marriage... no accidental shoot, copied?)

Is there any doubt which the Sword of the Spirit is, warrior? The combatant needs to know it in every detail, how it works, how much it weighs, how to load, caliber, how many rounds on the clip. You cannot leave home without it. On mission the combatant needs to use it very prudently, so as to neutralize positively identified targets, and not waste rounds. Saint Paul wrote in the end, the Sword of the Spirit is the Word of God. Did you understand where it is? On the Holy Bible, where else?

Choose your Bible carefully. Very carefully. For brief consultations you may use an electronic one, but for studying and engaging in combat it is important to have one in paper, that does not fail, does not break, does not depend on energy, and may receive your comments. Christian bibles are different than the ones used by the protestants, those do not have the books of Tobias and Judith, for example. Besides, some translations to your language have variations. I always use the Ave-Maria Bible and also the CNBB. Never consider biblical texts from low reliable Internet websites.

The Word of God is a valorous weapon when combating the enemy. First, it is much more powerful than words and gestures based just on your reason and intellect. Besides, its reach is much longer, the Word of God is the only way to open a breach on hearts hardened by sin. Have in mind that the enemy is not that poor sinner, but the devil acting through him. The victory of Christ is against sin, and it is against this enemy that we fight, to show the truth to a sinner and allow that God acts in that sinner.

The Bible should not be just read, or studied like if it was a school book. The good understanding of the biblical texts requires a praying attitude. Before anything else, begin with the sign of the cross and a praise, spoken or sung. If you do not know praising songs, read a Psalm and look for gospel music to listen daily. Start with the Gospels, then the

Letters of the Apostles, one chapter a day. Read once, think about it, read again. Writing a spiritual diary helps a lot.

"Where two or more be gathered in my name, there I will be". The Word must be shared to take effect. Therefore, the combatant shall start to talk about God with his wife, then the children, enlarge to relatives, close colleagues, but always very humbly. You should not say anything by your own intelligence, but by the action of the Holy Spirit through you.

The Sword of the Spirit only sustain itself if all the other items of the Armor are in good condition. Speaking of the life and teachings of Jesus while keeping a corrupt and promiscuous life is an empty speech, that may eventually convince the most desperate, but it is far from God. By the way, your dialogue with God must be continuous, every day and every hour are appropriate to talk to God and listen what He has to tell.

The Word of God does not manifest itself only by speaking or writing. Every gesture, attitude or labor that the combatant shows is a Christian testimony in life. More than being polite with everybody, with no distinction of social class or occupation, the combat that the Christian disputes encompasses avoiding colleagues at work who speak only foul language or pornography, stop using counterfeit products, and also respecting traffic laws and refusing all kind of undue favors.

I am writing a few examples of how the enemy does incursions in order to try to strike the combatant. When I was writing this book, I showed the draft to a Christian colleague in fatigues, and he said that its content was very strong, I would expose the problems of many soldiers. The answer came like a shot: "Blessed are you when they shall insult you and shall persecute you, because of my sake".Threat neutralized and confirmation that I am on the right track.

At parties I always refuse all kinds of alcoholic beverage, and in restaurants we only ask healthy plates (broccoli pizza, orange juice with carrot). When asked the reason, I say that "my body is the Temple of the Holy Spirit". I do not need any artificial substance in my brain to be happy. Because I don't watch soap operas nor read gossip magazines, at comments about that I answer: "the eyes are the light of the body"; if I don't consume garbage with the mouth, why would I consume it with the eyes and ears?

When somebody ask why I don't shout, don't speak foul language or swearing, to God or not, I tell him that "What goes into someone's mouth does not defile a man, but what comes out of their mouth, that is what defiles them". This is apparently in contradiction with the previous one, think about them and you will understand when using them.

When somebody ask why I volunteer to peace missions, among other military missions, at the border or in ghettos, even with all dangers and discomfort, I answer at the same time: "Blessed are the peacemakers, for they will be called children of God". Not even my family can understand why I stay away from them for weeks, risking my life for unknown people and many times ungrateful, selfish and exploiter. Many of them have never heard of Jesus, or do not believe in Him.

Sometimes they ask why I have a common car, a common house, go to work by bicycle even when it rains, don't have a brand new smartphone and don't wear brand clothes, the answer is "no one can serve two masters, those who serve god Money cannot serve God". Because in conversations I never expose anything that has not been asked ("Why you didn't say you studied and served abroad, speak other languages, served with General Him?"), I just answer that "those who humble themselves will be exalted, and those who exalt themselves will be humbled". And when they start to point me my past sins, in order to disqualify the Work of God make through me, I return with "Take the plank out of your eye before you remove the speck from your brother's eye".

Many times people tried to show me pornographic images at the lodge, but I tell them that "those who desire another woman, even in his heart, has already committed adultery". And when they imply that my wife boss me too much, I return the fire with "love your wives just as Christ loved his Church", in other words, with extreme sacrifice.

They also told me that I deserve a better work, I have qualification to earn much more, without having to bear such a heavy burden. I answer that "I have to flourish where God planted me". If they start to inflate my ego with praises, be they true or false, I reply that "blessed are the humble, for they shall inherit the earth".

When I defend the observance of the dignity of the human being in operations, through the Rules of Engagement, *jus cogens* norms of Human Rights and/or International Law of the Armed Conflicts, I receive from some flustered people the label of disunited, stuck wheel, betrayer. The response is clear: "Blessed are those who are persecuted because of righteousness, for theirs is the Kingdom of Heaven". When someone ask me to take it easy on the soldier who committed some misconduct, I shoot "Blessed are those who hunger and thirst for righteousness, for they shall be satisfied".

When they speak about dissolution of marriages, I promptly answer that "what God has joined together, let not man separate". If they have not celebrated their matrimony at the Church, or have different ephemeral relationships, I tell that "he who gives himself to his passions, like the horse and the donkey, the devil has power over".

When they put in check my faith in Jesus Christ, the Catholic Church, and in Our Lady, I remember the words of Jesus to Saint Thomas: "Blessed are those who believe without seeing me". If someone starts to mutter about corruption, heat, traffic, cold, rain, lines, debts, work, investments, I say that "seek first the Kingdom of God and his righteousness, and all these things will be added to you".

There's no use in copying and repeating what I or somebody spoke. Understand this: it is not me who is speaking, but the Sword of the Holy Spirit that speaks through me. For my own strength only I would not do it, the persecution and humiliation are very strong, the fear, the shame, and the concupiscence would make me shrug and be quiet. I need to be authentic, or it is better not to say anything.

One more example: when they ask what I get with all that, what the gain is, what the advantage is, I answer: "Do not let my right hand know the charity that your left hand does. Then Your Father, who sees what is done in secret, will reward you with treasures in Heaven". The feeling of accomplished duty is more valuable than any stuff or advantage. Besides, I am very happy in keeping anonymity. When I disappear, the Work of God appears.

8. TIME FOR BATTLE

"If the world hates you, keep in mind that it hated me first. If you belonged to the world, it would love you as its own. As it is, you do not belong to the world, but I have chosen you out of the world. That is why the world hates you. Remember what I told you 'A servant is not greater than his master'. If they persecuted me, they will persecute you also. If they obeyed my word, they will obey yours also. They will treat you this way because of my name, for they do not know the one who sent me. If I had not come and spoken to them, they would have no sin, but now they have no excuse for their sin. If I had not done among them works which no one else did, they would not have sin; but now they have both seen and hated Me and My Father as well. But this is to fulfill what is written in their Law: they hated me without reason". John 15, 18 to 25.

Combatant, you can bring the Light of the World where it is needed. Do not hide your capacity to sanctify yourself and your family, and also to bring back the Lord's stray sheep back to the flock. Jesus is the Good Shepperd. He knows His sheep by name, and they recognize His voice. The Good Shepperd gives His life to His sheep. Follow His example. "Renounce self, take up his cross and follow me".

The Christian combatant fears God, and no one else. However, listen to the opinion of Christian relatives and friends, not always our discernment is well tuned. As a leader of your family, you are the head, the first to jump from the helicopter, the first to disembark, the first to face the enemy. Who likes to be the first in a free fall parachuting at night? Release yourself to God with all your body and soul. "Hold the hand of God and go".

During school term I was very shy, spoke little, had just a few friends. Because I did not drink nor spoke foul words, they produced a *jingle* where I joined hands, prayed and said Amen. They barely knew my childhood full of pornography, lies and falsehoods. Just one example: when I was seven I managed to cheat my mother so she would do the math homework for me, and the teacher found out because her handwriting is much more beautiful than mine. There was a lot of unconfessed sin and a lot of unresolved hurt, but it was all kept. When I left college, I went through moments of intense temptation, of putting everything into practice.

As I became closer to God, temptation increased more and more. Which were my weak spots? First, the fact that I have always seen the female segment as an object of consumption, since my childhood. My dating and engagement time were not the least saint, and I ended up bringing all these behaviors to the matrimony. Lack of dialogue and empathy were always the fuel for discussions. All that sinfulness was accumulated, I had no courage to put into practice neither to confess it.

Several people helped me exiting the vicious cycle of sin, but the most important one was my wife, who taught me the value of working and studying, and then I stopped bumming around and studied with dedication all the college subjects, then for public job contests. My vainglory was gone, I apologized for everything, even for things I wasn't guilty of. My laziness and vanity gave place to work in a number of areas, as a bricklayer assistant, English teacher, lawyer and finally a soldier. Just the gluttony and lust remained, the ones I consider most difficult.

Slowly I learned how to fast. My first fasting was of sweetener, during Lent. It wasn't the least easy to drink anything bitter. I liked it so much that nowadays I happily drink black coffee with lemon juice. Later on there were other fastings during Lent, of rice, milk, always carefully substituting by others with similar nutritional value. A few times I did fasting of lunch, but it was not easy to do the home-work-home track by bike when fasting, I sinned later eating too much.

Penance is different than fasting. Both are a mortification of the body, but fasting is the absence of eating, and penance is an effort of the body (going to the gym is not penance!). It is similar to Meal-Ready-to-Eat or field ration: if you eat, it's penance; if you don't, it's fasting.

The penance to overcome lust was more uphill. It required the end of pornography and masturbation, after confession and reconciliation. My wife had a lot of patience with me, as I had with her. It was a common effort to rediscover sanctity in marriage, specially fertility. No more vasectomy or contraceptives, we use the Billings method. We have been blessed with two girls, and if we have more it will be a blessing. "Anyone who welcomes a little child like this welcomes me". If the marriage is not open to life, through children, is neither open to God.

The engagement in spiritual battle may occur anytime, anywhere. One day I was leaving the bakery and I found two boys asking for money, saying they were hungry and wanted to eat something. I have already seen them before, smoking something different than filtered cigarettes, in front of the near church. I had no doubts. "I saw you two taking drugs right there, and now you ask me for money?". They denied vehemently. "Get rid of drugs, they are killing you". I have never seen them again, at the bakery or smoking in front of the church. *Head shot* on the enemy.

In more than one opportunity I saw people throwing used paper on the floor. I took the paper, went to them and said: "You dropped this paper". That was a good opportunity to experience love to the neighbor. Despite the fact they were ashamed of being caught doing something wrong, I gave them the opportunity to redeem themselves. If they threw again the paper on the floor, it does not matter to me.

Choose well who you are going to serve. "For whoever wants to save his life will lose it, but whoever loses his life for me will find it". We are in this world, with all the problems inside us, the sin. Those that apparently are outside us are inside somebody, and it's not up to us to judge the sins of others. "With the measure you use it will be measured to you".

You aren't here to judge, but to help saving. That way you will be saved. Simple like that, like all God's stuff must be.

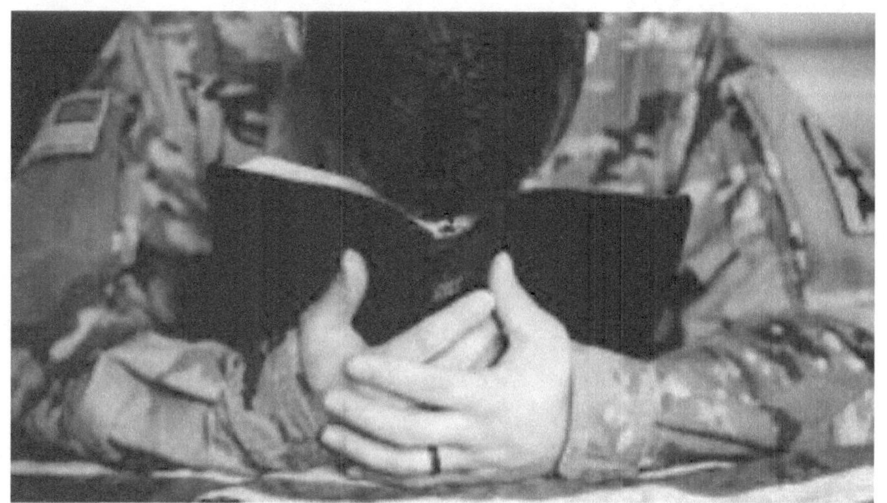

CONCLUSION

"The eleven disciples went to Galilee, to the mountain where Jesus had ordered them. When they saw him, they worshiped him, but some doubted. Then Jesus came to them and said: "All authority in heaven and on earth has been given to me. Therefore go and make disciples of all nations, baptizing them in the name of the Father and of the Son and of the Holy Spirit and teach them to obey everything I have commanded you. And surely I am with you always, even unto the end of the world" Matthew 28, 16 to 20.

The Christian is not of this world, does not belong to this world. Believing in Jesus and following His Word is seen as madness by those who live by the rules of the world. This sort of spiritual combatant joins a detachment commissioned to accomplish a mission, determined by God due to His love for His Creation. We are all soldiers on command of Our Lord Jesus Christ, each one in his expertise, but always keeping in mind the mission.

Maybe you were able to valiantly arrive here, reader, but you may still have doubts about that more active position of the catholic in relation to the world around him, the need to engage himself in the spiritual combat. Do not be conformed to this world, but be transformed by the renewing of your mind, wrote Saint Paul to the Romans.

Saint Pius X, in his Catechism, let it even clearer: "The Confirmation, or Chrism, is a Sacrament that gives us the Holy Spirit, imprints on our souls **the mark of a soldier of Jesus Christ**, and makes us perfect Christians" (Catechism, 575). Didn't you know? Too late, now you do. Confirmed as truly Christians we receive the gifts of the Holy Spirit, the fire support needed to the battle against our only enemy.

The spiritual seal that Confirmation brings is rich in significance: it's a sign of abundance, joy, purification and beauty, but also agility (anointing of the athletes and fighters) and healing (it alleviates bruises and helps healing wounds) (CIC, 1293).

Each of the infused gifts of the Holy Spirit is intimately linked to a human virtue (usual and strong disposition to do good, that's why it's essential to always practice virtue (it depends only on you) and in difficult times the Holy Spirit acts, doing the impossible from the moment you do everything possible. It's similar to when you are rowing on open sea and, when a shark shows up, a fierce wind starts to push you to land.

Below are the virtues and respective gifts, and a very short explanation:

Virtue of Faith – Gift of Understanding

Saint Thomas Aquinas, at the age of six, asked to a priest: "Who is God?", "You don't need to understand", answer the priest, "this is about faith". "But it's exactly because I have faith in God that I want to understand Him"

In Catholic doctrine, the Virtue of Faith and the Gift of Understanding are complementary concepts, but they have important differences. Faith, a theological virtue, is a habitual disposition that leads us to believe in God and in all that He has revealed. It is a free response of the human being to divine revelation, which allows us to trust in the truths that we cannot fully understand with reason alone.

On the other hand, the Gift of Understanding is one of the gifts of the Holy Spirit. He grants us the ability to understand more deeply the truths revealed by God. While Faith leads us to believe, the Gift of Understanding helps us to understand these truths more clearly and deeply, facilitating a more intimate relationship with God and a greater understanding of His will.

In short, the Virtue of Faith is the habitual disposition to believe in God, while the Gift of Understanding is a grace that helps us to better understand these truths. Both are essential in the Christian life: Faith sustains us in hope and trust, and the Gift of Understanding deepens this relationship, allowing us to know more about God and His work.

Virtue of Hope – Gift of Knowledge

"Wait, oh my soul, wait. Ignores the day and hour (...) the more you struggle, the more you will prove the love you have to your God and the more you will be joyful one day with your Beloved One, in such a happiness and excitement that can never end", Saint Teresa of Jesus (of Avila)

The Virtue of Hope is one of the three theological virtues, along with Faith and Charity. It is a habitual disposition that leads us to desire and confidently hope for eternal life and the promises of God. According to Catholic doctrine, hope sustains the heart of the Christian, even in the face of difficulties and suffering, because it believes in the faithfulness of God and in the fulfillment of His promises.

This virtue is not just a feeling of optimism, but a firm confidence that, with God's grace, we can achieve salvation and the fullness of life. Hope motivates the Christian to persevere in faith, to seek holiness and to remain firm in the face of adversity, always trusting in divine mercy.

On the other hand, the Gift of Knowledge is one of the gifts of the Holy Spirit that enables the believer to know the truths of God and His creation. This gift does not refer only to intellectual knowledge, but to a deep and spiritual understanding of divine and human realities, which leads to admiration and love for God.

The Gift of Knowledge helps Christians discern what is true, good, and beautiful, guiding their actions and decisions according to God's will. It enlightens the mind, allowing believers to perceive God's presence in the world and in their own lives, promoting a broader understanding of the divine mystery.

Although distinct, the Virtue of Hope and the Gift of Knowledge complement each other on the spiritual journey. Hope provides the motivation and confidence needed to persevere in faith, even without fully understanding God's mysteries. It sustains the Christian's heart in the search for salvation.

The Gift of Knowledge offers knowledge that deepens this hope, clarifying God's truths and strengthening faith with understanding.

While hope keeps one's eyes on the future and God's promise, the Gift of Knowledge helps one perceive God's presence in the present, nurturing trust and love.

In Catholic doctrine, the Virtue of Hope and the Gift of Knowledge play essential roles in the life of Christians. Hope is the foundation that sustains trust in divine mercy, while the Gift of Knowledge enlightens the mind, allowing a deeper understanding of the mystery of God. Together, they lead the faithful to a fuller and more conscious relationship with the Creator, promoting a journey of faith based on trust and knowledge.

Virtue of Charity – Gift of Wisdom

"If we get away from evil because of the punishment, we are slaves; if we seek good for the reward, we are mercenaries; if it is for the good in itself, and for the love of who is commanding that we obey, then we are in the situation of children", Saint Basilio

In the spiritual life of a Christian, the search for a deeper union with God and with others is supported by various virtues and gifts of the Holy Spirit. Among these, the Virtue of Charity and the Gift of Wisdom stand out. Although they have distinct functions, they complement each other in the journey of faith, helping the believer to truly love and understand the mystery of God.

The Virtue of Charity, also known as love, is considered the greatest of the theological virtues. It is a habitual disposition that leads the Christian to love God above all things and his neighbor as himself. According to Catholic doctrine, charity is the love that manifests itself in concrete actions, seeking the good of others without expecting a reward.

Charity is the heart of the Christian life, because it reflects God's love for us and invites us to love selflessly. It manifests itself in mercy, compassion, patience and the giving of oneself for others. This virtue transforms the way of life, becoming an expression of divine love in daily practice.

On the other hand, the Gift of Wisdom is one of the gifts of the Holy Spirit that enables us to perceive and value the things of God with a deep understanding. It helps us to see reality in the light of faith, recognizing the presence of God in all things and valuing what is true, good and beautiful.

Wisdom is not limited to intellectual knowledge, but involves an experience of love and union with God. It leads us to a deeper understanding of the divine mystery, helping us to discern what is most important in life and to guide our actions according to God's will.

Although distinct, the Virtue of Charity and the Gift of Wisdom are intrinsically linked in the life of a Christian. Charity is the love that manifests itself in concrete actions, while wisdom is the understanding that helps us to love more deeply and truly.

Wisdom enlightens the mind, allowing us to perceive the presence of God in everything around us, awakening in us a more genuine and selfless love. Charity leads us to put this love into practice, living in a way that reflects God's love for all humanity.

In Catholic doctrine, the Virtue of Charity and the Gift of Wisdom are essential for a full and authentic life of faith. Charity teaches us to truly love, while wisdom helps us to understand God's love and apply it in our actions. Together, they form a path of spiritual growth, leading the Christian to a deeper union with God and with others, based on true love and an understanding of the divine mystery.

Virtue of Prudence – Gift of Counsel

"The prudent gives thought to his steps" Proverbs 14,15

The Church teaches that we have virtues and gifts from the Holy Spirit that help us on our earthly pilgrimage. Among them are the Virtue of Prudence and the Gift of Counsel. Although they have distinct functions, both work together to guide our actions and decisions, promoting a life more aligned with God's love and will.

Prudence is one of the cardinal virtues, considered essential in the moral life of a Christian. It is the ability to discern what is right and act sensibly, prudently and justly. According to Catholic doctrine, prudence helps us to evaluate circumstances, weigh the consequences of our actions and choose the best path to follow.

This virtue is like a beacon that illuminates our decisions, preventing impulses and hasty actions. It encourages us to reflect, seek advice when necessary and act with moderation, always seeking the greater good and God's will. Prudence, therefore, is a virtue that accompanies us in all areas of life, helping us to live responsibly and wisely.

On the other hand, the Gift of Counsel is one of the gifts of the Holy Spirit that grants us special guidance in decision-making. It helps us discern God's will for our lives, offering an inner guidance that leads us to choices that promote spiritual and moral good.

Counsel is not just an opinion, but a divine help that guides us to act with prudence, love and justice. It enables us to hear the voice of God in our hearts, to seek counsel in prayer, in the Church and in the community, and to make decisions that are aligned with the values of the Gospel. Thus, the Gift of Counsel is a light that illuminates the path, especially in times of doubt or difficulty.

Although distinct, the Virtue of Prudence and the Gift of Counsel complement each other in the life of the Christian. Prudence is the virtue that prepares us to act wisely, while the Gift of Counsel is the divine guidance that helps us choose the best path according to God's will.

Prudence gives us the ability to assess situations with maturity, while Counsel helps us to perceive which decision is most aligned with God's plan for our lives. Together, they form a powerful duo that leads us to wise, just, and loving actions.

In the journey of faith, the Virtue of Prudence and the Gift of Counsel are essential to living responsibly and in alignment with God's will. Prudence teaches us to act with wisdom and responsibility, while Counsel guides us to discern God's will in our choices. When they work together, they help us to make decisions that promote spiritual good, strengthening our relationship with God and with others. May we always seek this divine wisdom to walk with confidence and love on the path of the Lord.

Virtue of Justice – Gift of Piety

"Masters, provide your slaves with what is right and fair, because you know that you also have a Master in heaven", Colossians 4,1

In the Christian life, seeking moral perfection and union with God involves practicing virtues and receiving gifts from the Holy Spirit. Among these, the Virtue of Justice and the Gift of Piety stand out. Although they have distinct functions, both are essential for a life of authentic faith, promoting love, mercy and harmony in human relationships and with God.

Justice is one of the cardinal virtues, considered fundamental in the moral life of a Christian. It consists of giving each person what is due to them, promoting equity, honesty and respect for the laws and the rights of others. According to Catholic doctrine, justice is the foundation of human relationships, as it ensures that actions are guided by truth, social justice and solidarity.

Practicing justice means acting with integrity, defending the rights of others and promoting the common good. This virtue invites us to be fair in our attitudes, to respect differences and to always seek equity, reflecting God's love in our daily lives.

On the other hand, the Gift of Piety is one of the gifts of the Holy Spirit that leads us to a filial and loving relationship with God. It helps us recognize God as our loving Father and develop an attitude of reverence, respect, and devotion. Piety inspires us to love God with all our heart, with sincerity and gratitude, and to demonstrate this love through acts of mercy and care for others. Piety also motivates us to cultivate an attitude of humility, trust, and gratitude, recognizing God's presence in our lives and in the lives of others. It is a virtue that leads us to live with a heart full of love and reverence, promoting harmony between our relationship with God and with the people around us. Although distinct, the Virtue of Justice and the Gift of Piety complement each other in the journey of faith. Justice ensures that our actions are correct and fair, promoting respect and the common good. Piety, on the other hand, helps us to cultivate a loving and reverent relationship with God, which is also manifested in care and mercy for others. Justice without mercy can become cold or impersonal, while mercy without justice can turn into sentimentality or complacency. Together, these virtues and gifts form a balance that leads us to act with righteousness, love, and mercy, reflecting the heart of God in our lives.

In Catholic doctrine, the Virtue of Justice and the Gift of Mercy are essential for a full life aligned with God's will. Justice guides us to act with equity and integrity, while mercy leads us to love and reverence God and our neighbor. When cultivated together, these virtues help us live with responsibility, love, and mercy, building a more just society and a heart more filled with divine love. May we always seek this harmony to walk with faith, hope, and love on the path.

Virtue of Courage – Gift of Fortitude

"The Lord is my strength and song", Psalms 118,14

"In this world you will have tribulation, but take heart: I have overcome the world" John 16,33

In our journey of faith, we face many challenges and obstacles that require strength, courage and endurance from us. The Catholic Church teaches us that, to overcome these difficulties, we rely on virtues and gifts of the Holy Spirit that strengthen us and help us persevere. Among these, the Virtue of Courage and the Gift of Fortitude stand out. Although they have different functions, both work together to give us courage and firmness to follow God's path with confidence and hope.

Courage is one of the cardinal virtues, essential in the moral life of a Christian. It enables us to face fear, difficulties and temptations with firmness and determination. According to Catholic doctrine, courage helps us not to retreat in the face of evil, to persevere in faith and to act bravely, even when the path is difficult.

Practicing courage means not letting ourselves be dominated by fear, but trusting in God's strength to overcome obstacles. It is the virtue that drives us to defend truth, justice and our faith, even in times of adversity. Thus, courage is a virtue that strengthens us internally, allowing us to move forward with hope and confidence in God's promise.

On the other hand, the Gift of Fortitude is one of the gifts of the Holy Spirit that grants us spiritual strength and endurance. It helps us to remain firm in our faith, especially in times of trial, suffering or temptation. Fortitude gives us the courage to endure difficulties without losing hope or trust in God.

This gift enables us to resist temptations, to face adversity with serenity and to persevere in doing good. It is a divine help that sustains us, strengthening our soul and giving us the courage to move forward, even when everything seems difficult. Fortitude is, therefore, an inner strength that comes from God to keep us firm in our Christian vocation.

Although distinct, the Virtue of Courage and the Gift of Fortitude complement each other in the life of a Christian. Courage is a virtue that we can cultivate through human effort, helping us to act bravely in the face of challenges. Fortitude is a gift from the Holy Spirit, a divine grace that sustains and strengthens us in difficult times.

Together, they form a powerful duo: courage drives us to act, while Fortitude sustains us in perseverance. The virtue of courage helps us take the first step and face our fears, while the gift of Fortitude gives us the strength to continue, even when the path becomes difficult. Thus, we can say that courage is the human impulse, and Fortitude is the divine support that sustains us on the journey.

In the Christian life, the Virtue of Courage and the Gift of Fortitude are essential for facing challenges with faith, hope, and love. Courage motivates us to act bravely, while Fortitude gives us the strength to persevere and resist temptations and difficulties. When they work together, these forces help us to live with firmness and confidence in God's promise.

Virtue of Temperance – Gift of Fearing God

"Go not after your lusts, but refrain yourself from your appetites",
Ecclesiastics 18, 30

Temperance is one of the four cardinal virtues and refers to the rational control over desires and passions, promoting balance in human actions. According to Saint Thomas Aquinas, it moderates sensual pleasures, helping the individual to avoid excesses and seek moderation in all aspects of life (Summa Theologiae, II-II, q. 141).

In practice, temperance manifests itself in the ability to enjoy the good things created by God without allowing oneself to be dominated by them. It favors a balanced life, promoting physical, mental and spiritual health. For Catholics, this virtue is fundamental to living a harmonious existence aligned with God's will.

On the other hand, the Gift of the Fear of God is one of the seven gifts of the Holy Spirit mentioned in the book of Isaiah (11:2-3). It should not be confused with servile fear or terror; it is a reverent and filial feeling before God, recognizing His greatness, holiness and authority.

The Gift of Fear of God leads the faithful to avoid sin out of love and respect for the Lord, fostering a relationship of trust and voluntary submission to His will. It sustains the moral life by awakening in the heart of the believer a deep sense of responsibility before God.

Although distinct in nature—one being a moral virtue acquired through human effort (cardinal virtue) and the other a gift granted by the Holy Spirit—both are essential for spiritual growth.

Temperance is cultivated through the exercise of human and divine virtues; the Gift of Fear is a free gift from the Holy Spirit. Temperance helps in moderating worldly desires; the Gift of Fear promotes a reverent attitude that avoids sin out of love for God. Temperance acts in the sphere of sensual appetites and material goods; the Gift of Fear acts in the inner disposition of respect and submission to the divine will.

In the full Christian life, these two realities complement each other. Temperance provides the practical means to control human passions, while the Gift of Fear keeps alive in the heart the awareness of God's presence and infinite power. Together, they help the faithful to avoid excesses and attitudes that could distance them from God.

The virtue of Temperance and the Gift of Fear of God represent two essential pillars in the moral formation of the Catholic Christian. While one promotes balance in human actions, the other sustains a filial relationship with God based on reverent respect. The development of these qualities contributes to a more holy, harmonious life, aligned with divine teachings.

Important detail: virtues must be used together, or none of them holds. As G. K. Chesterton wrote, if the virtues are isolated, they become crazy. Figure yourself practicing acts of courage with no prudence, or making justice without temperance, or working on charity unattached to faith and hope...

Concluding: what features does the combatant have? According to the prescribed at the art. 3rd of the Geneva Conventions concerning the Prisoners of War, in order to be considered a combatant the person must fulfill the following requirements:

1. Being part of a chain of command, in our case the chain of command is the Holy Trinity, the Holy Father the Pope, cardinals, bishops, priests, deacons and lay people, and it may include also a coordinator of your praying group and your ministry or pastoral.

2. Use a distinctive sign, in order to distinction from the population, essential for the combatants to know which troop they belong. It can be a medal, a scapular, a pendant or even a ring or bracelet, as long as they are blessed.

3. Carry weapons ostensibly. If the combatant is afraid of what other people will think if he is seen with a Holy Bible or a Rosary in his hands, unfortunately this combatant is not ready yet.

4. Follow the Laws and Customs of War, which is, to know and follow the Commandments of the Law of God, duly explained by Jesus Christ at the Sermon on the Mountain (Matthew 5, 6 and 7), besides the Catechism of the Church and the Rules of Life of your ministry or Community of Life.

Doubts, warrior? So, now for the debts. You received the Grace of God in your life so many times, the proper retribution is to do good to others, help saving people, contribute to His work. "Courage, I have overcome the world". Fight on the side of who has already won, and will continue to win the battle!!

POSTFACE – THE CHRISTIAN'S ARMOR CAMP

All very well in theory, but how can we put it into practice? How can we actually train men of good will to become spiritual fighters? Reading this book is a good start, but the prayer life of a warrior of God can be greatly refined if he is given a personal encounter with God, through a retreat that puts into practice everything that has been taught here.

A life of prayer is similar to training for combat, that is, it needs to be in the individual's blood, because it will be necessary precisely in critical moments, in the tribulations of life, that prayer will be most necessary.

However, know that calm seas do not make good sailors. No one will be able to form an identity as a soldier of Christ if they are protected by air conditioning, enjoying croissants and espressos and posting motivational texts and videos on social media.

"Useful military discipline is not learned, sir, in fantasy, dreaming, imagining or studying; but by seeing, dealing and fighting", wrote Luís de Camões to King Dom Sebastião. In short, fighting is learned by fighting, whether it's riding a bike or living in a straight line.

Thinking about putting all these ideas into practice, the Comunidade Família Santa in Goiânia/GO has been developing, since 2019, a spiritual retreat with physical activities, called Campo da Armadura do Cristão (although everyone calls it CAC), with lots of prayer, anointing of the Holy Spirit and tests based on each of the pieces of armor that Saint Paul described in Ephesians 6.

As with every retreat, it is essential that the participant participates with an open heart, otherwise God will not find space to act. At CAC it is the same thing, there is no point in arriving on the day afraid of what will happen or, even worse, wanting to compete and win against others. Your greatest adversary wants exactly that, for you to be discouraged by fear or to become intoxicated by putting others down.

You may be disappointed with me, but I cannot tell you here how the CAC retreat works in detail, otherwise you who have not yet participated in the event will be at a disadvantage, you will not have the surprise effect. What I can write are guidelines for participating well in everything.

The CAC retreat is only for men, confirmed or in the process of receiving this important sacrament. Confirmation or Chrism is the indelible sign of the Soldier of Christ, according to Saint Pius X. Women also have their retreats, it is nothing personal. But to form holy men we need to be among men only.

The proverb "As iron sharpens iron, so one man sharpens another" (Proverbs 27:17) means that, just as iron becomes sharper when rubbed against iron, so men are perfected and strengthened by interaction with others. The rust of the soul may require greater friction to be cleaned, and contact with nature, with the Word of God and the testimony of colleagues will provide this.

First, make a good confession and prepare your soul well (eventually, if you die during the retreat, your mortal sins will not lead you to eternal damnation, if they are well confessed...). Jokes aside, the Holy Spirit acts more easily on a contrite soul, and you will be able to feel the movements of the Third Person of the Trinity with fine tuning, a fact that only those who are in a state of grace are able to perceive.

Second, know that the physical activities of the CAC involve various physical efforts, such as long walks, short walks with a load, vertical techniques, orientation with topographic maps, day and night progression, reflex action shooting in a confined environment, all with a good dose of rusticity, like any camp worthy of the name.

But this does not prevent anyone from taking the CAC, since all the tests can be adapted according to the physiological reality of the student. But I can guarantee that people who are obese, have partial paralysis, partial blindness, diabetes, heart problems, ulcers, hemophilia, arthritis, epilepsy and other similar clinical conditions were able to do all the activities.

You don't have to be an athlete to go to the retreat, but if this is a fear that dominates your heart, it's time to take better care of yourself, with your diet, physical activity and good physical and mental health habits. How can you expect to be a family man at home if you are mired in addictions?

What to bring to the CAC retreat (individual equipment): closed clothing (long sleeves and pants), sneakers or combat boots, thermal shorts or swimming trunks (to prevent chafing), rosary beads, Bible, water bottle or similar, camping tableware, flashlight, matches, hygiene kit (toilet paper, wet wipes, foot powder, soap, shampoo, razor, hair comb, tweezers, flip-flops, towel), 2 or 3 changes of socks, complete change of clothes, insect repellent, sunscreen, first aid kit (bandage, gauze, antiseptic, anti-inflammatory, painkiller, electrolyte replacement powder). Put everything in a waterproof bag and that fits in a backpack. Also take a sleeping bag and/or thermal blanket, inside a plastic bag. Wet stuff will make your dog shiver.

Do not take a tent, food or weapons (firearms or knives) to the retreat, there is no need for them at all, they will only get in your way and take up space. Cell phones, car keys and electronic components will be kept in a safe place, to be returned at the end. Let your family know that you will not be available during the retreat.

Finally, from what I can tell you without revealing the details of the CAC to you, is that you will receive a wooden cross, measuring 50 cm x 30 cm. Carry this cross with all devotion, it symbolizes the greatest proof of a God of love who came to this world to die for our salvation.

It was for me. It was for you. Make it worth it.

BAMBOO!!!

###

My sincere thanks for having read this book. I hope comments and reviews at rogeriocietto@gmail.com

Read also:
<u>Combating the Good Combat – How to fight Terrorism with a Peacekeeping Mission</u>[1]
<u>Ecohouse – A Holistic Approach about Sustainable Living</u>[2]
<u>The Lion and the Dragon – a FICTIONAL tale about Economics and Politics</u>[3]
I regret to inform that I have no profile on Facebook, Twitter or any other social media.
God bless you.

---

1. https://www.smashwords.com/books/view/262924

2. https://www.smashwords.com/books/view/264895

3. https://www.smashwords.com/books/view/745239